21st
Century
Skills Library

POWER UP!

FROM WASTE TO ENERGY

BY ROBERT GREEN

Published in the United States of America by
Cherry Lake Publishing, Ann Arbor, Michigan
www.cherrylakepublishing.com

Content Adviser
Denise Heikinen, Sustainable Futures Institute, Michigan Technological University

Credits
Photos: Cover and page 1, ©Jim West/Alamy; page 4, ©INSADCO Photography/
Alamy; page 7, ©Oplantz/Dreamstime.com; page 8, ©Rpernell/Dreamstime.com;
page 10, SergioZ, used under license from Shutterstock, Inc.; page 11, ©Urban
Zone/Alamy; page 12, ©The Natural History Museum/Alamy; page 15, ©Peter
Bowater/Alamy; page 16, ©mycola, used under license from Shutterstock, Inc.;
page 17, ©Dualcore/Dreamstime.com; page 18, ©Evron/Dreamstime.com; page 20,
©Psamtik/Dreamstime.com; page 23, ©David Colbran/Alamy; page 24, ©Uko_jesita/
Dreamstime.com; page 27, ©Kitigan/Dreamstime.com; page 29, ©Elena Elisseeva,
used under license from Shutterstock, Inc.

Library of Congress Cataloging-in-Publication Data
Green, Robert, 1969–
   From waste to energy / by Robert Green.
      p. cm.—(Power up!)
   Includes index.
   ISBN-13: 978-1-60279-509-9
   ISBN-10: 1-60279-509-6
   1. Recycling (Waste, etc.)—Juvenile literature. 2. Recycling (Waste,
etc.)—Environmental aspects—Juvenile literature. I. Title. II. Series.
   TD794.5.G74 2009
   333.793'8—dc22   2008045235

Cherry Lake Publishing would like to acknowledge
the work of The Partnership for 21st Century Skills.
Please visit *www.21stcenturyskills.org* for more information.

POWER UP!

TABLE OF CONTENTS

GENERATING ENERGY
HOW WASTE TO ENERGY

CHAPTER ONE
IS WASTE REALLY USELESS?

There is a smelly place in every home. Many people try not to think about. What is it? The garbage can!

Garbage looks gross, but it might be more useful than you think!

Garbage cans hold the things people don't want. After the yogurt is eaten, the container ends up in the trash. After newspapers are read, they land in the trash. When we cook, we throw away many parts of our meats, fruits, and vegetables.

Trash is household waste. It is the stuff people no longer find useful. What good is an empty yogurt container, a banana peel, or a newspaper that has already been read? The answer might surprise you.

Trash is one thing that people are always taking out of their homes. But what if we could turn the trash that we throw out of the house into something valuable that we bring into the house? That thing is **electricity**. It powers alarm clocks that buzz in the morning. It powers lights to read newspapers by. It powers the refrigerator that keeps food from spoiling in the heat.

Imagine using household waste to create electricity, something we use every day. Then trash would no longer be useless.

Scientists have discovered a way to turn waste into energy by burning it. When trash is burned, energy stored inside the trash is released in the form of heat. That heat can be used to make electricity. The electricity then travels from a **power plant** to houses and other buildings. It travels on electrical lines that connect the buildings to the power plant. This network of lines is known as a **power grid**. This is how **electrical energy** is shared through a community.

21ˢᵗ CENTURY CONTENT

Some businesses reuse their own waste to create energy for their factories. Kraft is a company that makes cheese and other food products. It turns some of its leftover food products into **natural gas**. The gas is then used to create electricity.

Why do companies want to turn their waste into energy? It is expensive to haul away waste in trucks. And trucks create air pollution in the form of a gas called carbon dioxide. Creating energy from waste makes good business sense and helps save the environment.

Burning trash is just one way to create electrical energy. It is, however, one of the least common sources of electricity. The most commonly burned substance in electrical power plants is **coal**. Sometimes **oil** is burned. Natural gas can also be used to produce electricity.

Coal, oil, and natural gas are limited resources. But trash seems to pile up all the time. Let's learn more about turning all that useless garbage into useful energy.

Coal provides more than 40 percent of the world's electricity.

CHAPTER TWO
WHERE DOES IT ALL GO?

Humans produce more and more trash every year. Household trash is most plentiful in the United States. As of 2005, the average person produced about 4.5 pounds

Sanitation workers use garbage trucks to drive through neighborhoods and collect trash.

(2 kilograms) of trash each day. That adds up to millions of tons of garbage each year just in the United States. Where does it all go?

Sanitation workers drive trucks from house to house and pick up garbage. In some places, people bring their trash directly to a dump and drop it off. At a dump, garbage is sorted. Metals, paper, plastics, and glass are often separated from other household trash. They are stored separately. Can you think of why?

Those items can be used again in a process known as **recycling**. Recycling takes glass from used glass bottles and turns it into new glass bottles. Recycling helps prevent trash from piling up by reusing the materials to form new objects.

LEARNING & INNOVATION SKILLS

When trash is buried in a landfill, it slowly breaks down, or decomposes. The decomposing trash gives off a gas known as methane. Scientists can capture the methane and use it to generate electricity or heat. Can you think of any other benefits of collecting the methane? Hint: Methane is harmful to the environment.

The rest of the trash is taken to landfills. A landfill is a place where trash is buried in the ground to decay over time. Landfills are usually located far from where most people live. Living near piles of trash would be unpleasant.

People are producing more trash every year. In 1960, Americans threw away about 2.6 pounds (1.2 kg) of trash per person every day. Today, we throw away almost twice that much. The trash is piling up in landfills, and many landfills are

Tons of waste are dumped in landfills every day.

Some communities have special bins for collecting each kind of recyclable trash.

full. It is becoming more and more difficult to find places to dump garbage.

Recycling is one solution. About 30 percent of trash in the United States is recycled every year. Another 14 percent of trash is burned to produce energy. Still, more than half of all garbage is placed in landfills, where it continues to pile up.

CHAPTER THREE
GETTING ENERGY FROM WASTE

The way garbage is turned into electricity is pretty remarkable. To understand the process, you need to know one of the basic laws of energy. The law is: energy cannot be created or destroyed. It just changes form. So, in this case, the energy needed to produce electricity from trash is already in the

Sometimes fossils take the form of an image left behind in the rock.

trash. In other words, energy is not *created* from the trash. Instead, energy is *released* from the trash.

But how does energy get trapped inside garbage in the first place? The answer requires us to look back in time. Most of the stuff that humans use for energy comes from a process that takes place over millions of years. That process is the hardening of once-living plants and animals into fossils. This happens when the remains of plants and animals are covered by layers of rock and dirt. After millions of years, these fossils are full of useful energy. Coal and oil are the two most common forms of fossil fuels. When they are burned, their energy is released as heat.

LEARNING & INNOVATION SKILLS

Fossil fuels such as coal and oil are nonrenewable sources of energy. That means they can't be made again in a short amount of time. Solar energy and wind energy are renewable forms of energy. They can be replaced in short periods of time.

Do you think that waste is a renewable or nonrenewable form of energy? Why?

Let's use plastic garbage as an example. The same energy trapped inside fossil fuels is found in plastics that we throw out every day. How is that possible? It is because plastics are made from oil. So they contain within them the fossil fuel energy of the oil.

To get energy from trash, it is burned in an **incinerator** at an electrical power plant. The energy from the trash is released in the form of heat. This is known as thermal energy. That energy is used to heat pipes that pump water around the hot incinerator. When the water is heated, it turns into a gas known as steam.

Steam takes up more volume than the water in the pipes, so it causes pressure. The pressure that builds up in the pipes is directed toward a machine that spins. This machine is called a **turbine**. The spinning of the turbine causes a reaction that produces electrical energy. This completes the final step in the creation of energy.

The electrical energy travels away from the power plant over a series of wires on the power grid. The electricity travels quickly along power lines. The electricity must be slowed down to make it usable in houses, factories, and other buildings. **Transformers** are used to slow it down. These machines make the electricity much less dangerous. The last step in the process is a single line that runs from a power line to a house or another building. This single line connects

A turbine is like a big fan. As steam moves through the its blades, the turbine spins.

the user of electricity with the distant power plant where the electricity was generated.

It is important to remember that trash is just the starting point. Burning trash is what starts the rest of the process in a power plant. Burning trash to create energy does two things: it creates electricity and it gets rid of those smelly piles of trash. In the United States, however, only 0.4 percent of

Electricity passes through power substations on its way to homes and other buildings.

Power lines are everywhere. We use the energy they supply to run computers, televisions, and many other things.

electricity is created by burning trash. The most common source of fuel for power plants is still coal. Coal is fed into an incinerator just like waste. It is used to create about half of all the electricity used in the United States.

CHAPTER FOUR
THE GREAT DEBATE

You are probably thinking that burning trash for energy is a great idea. But some **environmentalists** aren't convinced. They say that burning garbage to create electricity

Toxins released by burning garbage can damage the air we breathe.

does more than reduce the amount of trash around. It also harms the environment. Are they right?

The answer is yes, to some degree. Burning trash can release harmful substances into the air. Imagine all the different things that end up in the trash—metals, plastics, rubber, and batteries. These all contain chemicals that are released when burned, which can poison the air. Many chemicals that are helpful to us when making plastics are harmful to us when they are released into the air or water. In other words, burning trash can cause pollution.

Still, many people support the idea of turning waste into energy. They argue that the fires that burn garbage destroy most of the chemicals that can pollute the air. Also, special chemicals called scrubbers are sprayed into the smoke released from burning trash. These scrubbers make many chemicals harmless. Complicated filters also help to keep harmful gases from going into the air and polluting the environment.

People who support burning trash for energy use other arguments, too. They point out that if the trash isn't burned, the harmful chemicals in trash sit in landfills. They say this may lead to soil and water pollution.

Something else makes the question of whether to burn trash even more complicated. Burning trash is expensive. Trash itself is very cheap. It can be found on every street corner. The costs begin when trucks are used to move trash to power plants. Those trucks need gasoline, which is expensive. Once at the power plant, costs skyrocket. The biggest expense is the technology to clean the pollutants out of the smoke released from burning garbage. This can cost more money than will be made by selling the electricity.

Burning trash leaves behind ash which must be disposed of properly. If it isn't, it can damage the environment.

Even after the trash is burned, an expense remains. Trash produces ash when it is burned at high temperatures. The ash is black dust that contains metals and toxins. They can be harmful to the environment. The ash must be dumped in special landfills. The landfills must prevent these pollutants from affecting the soil or water nearby.

Environmentalists have another argument against burning trash. Some say that burning trash will cause people to stop recycling. People will simply decide to throw everything into the same pile and burn it. But some things burn better than others. Metals, for example, are usually recycled rather than burned. A combination of recycling and burning may be the best way to reduce trash. This mixed approach has been adopted by many countries around the world.

21ST CENTURY CONTENT

Some common items that you might normally throw in the trash are better off being recycled. Set aside aluminum cans and glass bottles for recycling. This is an easy way to help cut down on the amount of trash that goes into landfills. If you live in a town that has a recycling program, encourage your friends and neighbors to separate their recyclables from the rest of their trash. If your town does not have a recycling program, write a letter to your local government. Explain why you think town leaders should start a recycling program. Your ideas could help make a big change in your community.

Workers at recycling centers separate plastic, glass, metal, and paper.

CHAPTER FIVE
ENVIRONMENTAL BALANCING ACT

The debate over whether or not to burn trash continues. As it does, we need to look at the larger problem. Humans create a tremendous amount of waste. We throw out old

We don't often think about how much trash we produce each day.

shoes, old mattresses, old cars, old televisions, and many bags of household trash. Remember, each person in the United States throws out an average of 4.5 pounds (2 kg) of trash every day.

Why do people produce so much trash? One part of the answer is that we live in a consumer society. Consumers are people who buy things. Buying things that are for sale keeps the economy moving. It means that people have jobs making and selling things. Think about the making and selling of bread. When we buy bread, it helps support the farmers who grow the grain that goes into it. It also supports the baker who makes the bread. Some of the cost of the bread goes to support the people who transport it from the bakery to the store. These are just a few of the jobs that are involved in making and selling bread. And bread is just one of the many products we use each day.

Each time we buy something, we are part of a long chain of activity. It is the basis of our economy. But with each purchase, there is waste. And that waste must go somewhere. When landfills become crowded with trash, new ones are needed. This means more valuable land is given over to garbage.

When people look at overflowing landfills, burning garbage seems like a good idea. It is expensive, but it will get rid of the trash. And if electricity can be created from burning garbage, the idea looks even better.

New technology is likely to shape the future debate over whether or not to burn waste for energy. We already have chemical treatments to make the smoke from burning trash less harmful. Even the ash is treated so that it does not harm the soil. Now scientists are working on ways to make burning waste for energy less expensive. Lowering the price would make the technology more common.

21ST CENTURY CONTENT

Trash can be a big business. Companies are paid to cart it away to dumps. Other companies make a profit by selling energy from trash. The key to making money from burning trash is technology. New methods for cleaning the air from burned trash can make waste-to-energy plants profitable. A company in South Africa, Prestige Thermal, opened the world's largest waste-to-energy plant in 2008. It is relying on new technology to make the energy less expensive to produce.

At the same time, people continue to look for ways to reduce the amount of trash they produce. Some people, for example, bring their own coffee mugs to coffee shops.

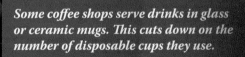

Some coffee shops serve drinks in glass or ceramic mugs. This cuts down on the number of disposable cups they use.

This way, they don't have to use—and throw away—paper coffee cups. Others bring reusable bags to the grocery store. This way, they won't use any plastic bags.

Even though people are working to cut down on the amount of trash they produce, garbage will still pile up. So what do you think? Does it make sense to burn waste for energy?

LIFE & CAREER SKILLS

Pay close attention to the packaging of the products you buy. It is one way to make an impact on the amount of trash in your local landfill. Avoid purchasing individually packaged items, such as bottles of juice. Instead, buy one large juice container and use it to refill a glass or a reusable drinking bottle.

You should also avoid items that are packaged using plastic. Plastic is much more harmful to the environment that other common packaging materials. Instead, try to buy more products that come in containers made of glass, paper, or cardboard. Each small choice you make about the products you buy can add up to make a big difference.

Using your own refillable water bottle instead of buying bottled water helps cut down on trash.

GLOSSARY

coal (KOHL) a black mineral formed from the remains of ancient plants; a fossil fuel

electrical energy (i-LEK-trih-kuhl EN-ur-jee) energy produced from a flowing electrical charge

electricity (i-lek-TRISS-uh-tee) a form of energy carried by wires to power homes and buildings

environmentalists (en-vye-ruhn-MEN-tal-ists) people who try to limit the harm of human activity on the environment

fossil fuels (FOSS-uhl FYOOLZ) substances, such as oil, coal, and natural gas, that are formed from the remains of ancient plants and animals

incinerator (in-SIN-uh-ray-tur) a furnace for burning trash

natural gas (NACH-ur-uhl GASS) gas that forms underground and can be burned for energy

oil (OYL) a thick, liquid fuel found underground

power grid (POU-ur GRID) the network of wires that carry electricity from power plants to buildings

power plant (POU-ur PLANT) a place where electricity is generated

transformers (transs-FOR-murz) devices that change the force of an electrical current

turbine (TUR-byn) machine with a rotor and blades driven by steam, water, hot gas, or air

FOR MORE INFORMATION

BOOKS

Fridell, Ron. *Earth-Friendly Energy*. Minneapolis: Lerner Publications, 2009.

Landau, Elaine. *The History of Energy*. Minneapolis: Twenty-First Century Books, 2006.

Orme, Helen. *Energy for the Future*. New York: Bearport Publishing, 2008.

Wilcox, Charlotte. *Earth-Friendly Waste Management*. Minneapolis: Lerner Publishing Group, 2009.

WEB SITES

EIA Energy Kid's Page: Waste-to-Energy
www.eia.doe.gov/kids/energyfacts/saving/recycling/ solidwaste/wastetoenergy.html
Learn facts about using waste as a source of energy

NIEHS Kids' Pages: Reduce, Reuse, and Recycle
kids.niehs.nih.gov/recycle.htm
Learn ways you can help cut down on the amount of trash you throw away

INDEX

ABOUT THE AUTHOR

Robert Green has written more than 30 books for students. He is a regular contributor to publications of the Economist Intelligence Unit and holds graduate degrees from New York University and Harvard.